Welcome to LIFESEARCH!

If you urgently need to prepare to lead a LIFESEARCH group, turn the page and read QUICKLEAD. QUICKLEAD will give you enough information to get started.

LIFESEARCH hopes to help you and other persons within a small group explore topics about which you are concerned in your everyday living. We've tried to make LIFESEARCH

✓ immediately helpful to you;

✓ filled with practical ideas;

✓ Christian-oriented and biblically based;

✓ group building, so you will find companions in your mutual struggles and learning;

✓ easy for anyone to lead.

You have probably chosen to join with others in studying this LIFESEARCH book because you feel some need. You may feel that need in your life strongly. Our hope for you is that by the time you complete the six chapters in this book with your LIFESEARCH group, you will have

✓ a better handle on how to meet the need you feel;

✓ some greater insights into yourself;

✓ a deeper understanding of how Christian faith can help you meet that need;

✓ a more profound relationship with God;

✓ new and/or richer relationships with the other persons in your LIFESEARCH group.

If you discover nothing else as part of this LIFESEARCH experience, we want you to learn this fact: *that you are not alone as you face life.* Other people have faced and still face the same problems, struggles, demands, and needs that you face. Some have advice to offer. Some have learned things the hard way— things they can now tell you about. Some can help you think through and talk through old concerns and new insights. Some can listen as you share what you've tried and what you want to achieve. Some even need what you can offer.

And you will never be alone because God stands with you.

The secret to LIFESEARCH is in the workings of your group. No two LIFESEARCH groups will ever be alike. Your LIFESEARCH group is made up of unique individuals—including you. All of you have much to offer one another. This LIFE-SEARCH book simply provides a framework for you and your group to work together in learning about an area of mutual concern.

We would like to hear what you think about LIFESEARCH and ways you can suggest for improving future LIFESEARCH books. A Mail-In Feedback survey appears in the back. Whether you lead the group or participate in it, please take the time to fill out the survey and mail it in to us.

IF YOU ARE LEADING A LIFE-SEARCH GROUP, please read the articles in the back of this book. These LIFESEARCH group leadership articles may answer the questions you have about leading your group.

IF YOU ARE PARTICIPATING IN A LIFESEARCH GROUP, BUT NOT LEADING IT, please read at least the article, "If You're Not Leading the Group." In any case, **you will benefit most if you come to your group meeting having read the chapter ahead of time and having attempted any assignments given in the previous chapter's "Before Next Time" sections.**

We want to remain helpful to you throughout your LIFESEARCH group experience. If you have any questions about using this LIFESEARCH book, please feel free to call Curric-U-Phone at 1-800-251-8591, and ask for the LIFESEARCH editor.

QUICKLEAD™

Look here for **QUICK** information about how to **LEAD** a session of LIFE-SEARCH. On LifeSearch pages, look for the following:

ICONS
Seven kinds of icons suggest different kinds of activities for your group to do at different points during the session (see page 4 for more information about ICONS).

MAIN TEXT: the "meat" of the session. Hopefully everyone will have read the MAIN TEXT ahead of time; if not, be prepared to offer a brief summary of the MAIN TEXT in your own words.

MARGINAL NOTES give you activity instructions and additional discussion starters.

CHAPTER THREE

LOOK BEYOND: WHAT DOES THE WORLD NEED NOW?

WORSHIP

Begin by praying this prayer:

O God of all people and places, we thank you for the marvelous diversity that you have created and placed in this world. We praise you for loving the world so much that you sent your son to be the light of this world. Inspire us to allow your loving light to shine in us and through us that the world might be transformed. In Christ's name, Amen.

CHECKING IN

Begin this session by welcoming any new persons to the group. Invite anyone to share significant events that may have occurred in their life since last time.

This time you will be looking beyond yourselves and the needs of persons in your congregation to the needs of persons in the world. Last time you were encouraged to visit a homeless shelter or community food pantry in your community or area. Or you may have visited a jail or talked with someone who works with the poor. These visits were intended to open your eyes to the needs of people in your area as you begin to reflect on how God wants to use your gifts for the transformation of the world into a community of justice and love.

DISCUSSION POINT

Debrief the members of the group on their visits using these questions and/or other questions as appropriate.

Spend some time reflecting on your visit to a shelter or food pantry. How many people does the shelter or pantry serve each month? Where do they get their resources? Where do they get their volunteers? Did you meet any of the clients of the shelter or pantry? How did you feel about being in such a setting? Does anyone in your group volunteer in ministries to the poor? What assistance does your church provide to the agencies that serve the poor? Has your church considered providing food or lodging for the poor? How does your congregation respond to emergency needs in your community? Who ministers to the needs of persons in jail or prison in your community? Has anyone in your congregation or community been on a short-term work-camp in this country or abroad? Has your community or area experienced a natural disaster such as a flood, earthquake, or hurricane? How did the church respond in that crisis? Are there any missionaries in your congregation or community who might reflect with you on the broader needs of our world? Please use these questions as a way to focus your attention on the needs of people beyond your own congregation.

If the group identifies such a missionary and wishes to do so, invite him or her to an extra session of your group to help members reflect about the needs around them.

SPIRITUAL GIFTS

UNDERLINED TEXT
identify discussion starters inside the MAIN TEXT.

For more information, read the **LEADERSHIP ARTICLES** in the back of this LIFESEARCH BOOK.

ICONS

ICONS are picture/symbols that show you at a glance what you should do with different parts of the main text at different times in the LifeSearch sessions.

The seven kinds of icons are

 WORSHIP—A prayer, hymn, or other act of worship is suggested at this place in the MAIN TEXT.

 CHECKING IN—At the beginning of each session, LifeSearch group members will be asked to "check in" with each other about what is happening in their lives. Sometimes group members will also be asked to "check in" about how their LifeSearch group experience seems to them.

 DISCUSSION POINT—Either the MAIN TEXT or a MARGINAL NOTE will suggest discussion starters. You will probably find more DISCUSSION POINTS than you can use in the usual LifeSearch session.

 GROUP INTERACTION—Either the MAIN TEXT or a MARGINAL NOTE will suggest a group activity that goes beyond a simple discussion within the whole group.

 BIBLE STUDY—At least once each session, your LifeSearch group will study a Bible passage together. Usually, DISCUSSION POINTS and/or GROUP INTERACTIONS are part of the BIBLE STUDY.

 WRITTEN REFLECTION—The MAIN TEXT will contain one or more suggestions for individuals to reflect personally on an issue. Space will be provided within the MAIN TEXT for writing down reflections. Sometimes individuals will be invited to share their written reflections if they wish.

 BEFORE NEXT TIME—In most sessions, your LifeSearch group members will be asked to do something on their own before the next time you meet together.

INTRODUCTION

This resource seeks to help persons within small groups identify and use the gifts God has given them for ministry to the needs of people in the church and in the world.

We find God's desires for our lives when we employ our spiritual gifts to meet the needs of people in our communities and in our world. Many books on spiritual gifts begin first by looking inside the individual to discover the gifts God has placed there and then by looking around in the world to determine where those gifts are needed. This resource reverses that approach. We will begin by examining the needs for ministry of people around us and only then will we look within to discover how the gifts for meeting those needs are already present in us.

We find God's will for our lives when we discover the place where the needs of the world and our gifts intersect. Imagine a line on which all the needs of the world are listed. Then imagine another line on which all of your gifts are written. Where those two lines cross is the place where we are called to serve. This resource seeks to help us assess both the needs of persons around us as well as to discover the gifts within so that we can be God's healing agents in a world of human need.

The New Testament tells us that God gives gifts to Christians for the transformation of life in this world. Spiritual gifts are not given by God to be hoard-ed and protected as merely personal possessions. Rather God bestows them on us for the service of people in the church and in the world.

In Paul's teaching on spiritual gifts in 1 Corinthians 12, he makes clear that while there are a variety of gifts and each is important, all gifts exist to serve other persons in some way. In speaking about the gifts of the Spirit, Paul writes: "To each is given the manifestation of the Spirit for the common good" (1 Corinthians 12:7). In Ephesians 4 Paul also points out that God's gifts are given for the service of others: "The gifts he gave were . . . to equip the saints for the work of ministry, for building up the body of Christ" (Ephesians 4:11-12). As we look at and talk about these things together, we shall first ponder what is needed "for the common good" and to build up the body of Christ. Then we shall explore the gifts God has placed within us to accomplish these ministries.

The author of 1 Peter also emphasizes that good stewards of God's gifts use those gifts in the service of others. "Like good stewards of the manifold grace of God, serve one another with whatever gift each of you has received" (1 Peter 4:10). Anyone who does not use his or her gift for the service of others is not being a good steward of that gift.

We too often see spiritual gifts as a purely personal possession. This indicates an attitude of superiority in the faith rather than the attitude that God's gift is to be offered wherever needed for the service of others. Consequently, we will discuss the communal context of spiritual gifts and how those gifts may be used to build up the body of Christ for the transformation of the world.

Most studies focus on Paul's discussion of spiritual gifts in Romans 12:10-8, 1 Corinthians 12:1-31, Ephesians 4:1-6, and the discussion in 1 Peter 4:10-11. Charles Bryant in his book *Rediscovering Our Spiritual Gifts* (Upper Room, 1991) and Kenneth Kinghorn in his book *Gifts of the Spirit* (Abingdon, 1976) do a thorough job of reflecting on these passages and their implications for discovering our spiritual gifts. However, in this resource we focus instead on some of the teachings of Jesus in the Gospels and their implications for using our gifts to meet the deepest needs of people around us. We find the guidance we need to discover and use our spiritual gifts not only in the teachings of Paul, but in the teachings of Christ himself.

Jesus did not declare that he had a gift for healing and then go out into the world to find someone to heal. Rather, persons with the need for healing appeared as Jesus travelled about the country. Then Jesus opened his life to God, and God brought forth the gifts for healing. In a similar way, in the first three chapters of this resource, we will focus on the needs of people who appear in the church and world around us. Then, in the last three chapters, we will look within ourselves to discover the gifts God has given us to meet those needs.

I believe and have experienced that when persons discover how their particular gifts bring life and hope to others, they are personally spiritually renewed. They live with the conviction that God is using them to make a difference in the world. My prayer for you is that you find fulfillment and meaning in your life. God eagerly anticipates your discovery of these treasures within, and God wants to use them for the transformation and redemption of the world.

—Kent Millard

Dr. Kent Millard is the Senior Pastor of St. Luke's United Methodist Church in Indianapolis. He has previously served congregations in South Dakota and Massachusetts. He received a Master of Divinity degree from Boston University School of Theology and a Doctor of Ministry degree from McCormick Theological Seminary in Chicago. Dr. Millard has served as a member of the leadership team for the Academy of Spiritual Formation program sponsored by The Upper Room. He and his wife, Minnietta are the parents of two children, Kendall and Koretta, and have one grandchild, Terrae.

CHAPTER ONE

LOOK WITHIN: WHAT DO I NEED?

WORSHIP

When the group is ready to begin, open with this prayer or one in your own words.

Begin your preparation for this session by praying this prayer:

O God, we thank you for bringing this specific group of persons together at this time and in this place. Thank you for each person here and for the way you will use each of us in ministry in this group and to others outside this group. Help us to be open to your leading through prayer, Scripture, and sharing. In Christ's name. Amen.

CHECKING IN

If you have a chalkboard or newsprint available, write down the reasons why persons have chosen to be a part of this study group. Record this information so that you can come back to it at the end of the study to determine to what degree expectations have been met.

The gathering time helps build community and encourages a climate for open and honest sharing. At this time each session you will get to know other members by sharing events of the past week or by sharing research you or other individual members may have done for a group topic.

For this first meeting be prepared to share in turn (1) your name; (2) brief information about your family, work, and leisure activities; and (3) why you have chosen to be a part of this group.

DISCUSSION POINT

What do you think about this approach?

Before we begin to identify and cultivate our own spiritual gifts, we will recognize how others have often used their spiritual gifts to minister to our needs. When we experience the ways in which God has used others to minister to us we become better able to recognize God's ways with us and how God is seeking to use our gifts in ministry.

Several years ago when our daughter was in high school, she became pregnant. As her parents we had feelings of pain for her, disappointment, failure, anxiety about the future, and concern over how the church I served as pastor would respond. In the midst of our pain, a lay couple in the church whom we had not known very well called and invited us to lunch. When we got together, they shared that they had gone through a similar situation several years earlier and knew some of the agony that we were going through. They shared their own feelings of pain, disappointment, failure, anxiety, and concern, and they shared how others in the church had helped them through that stressful time in their lives. They affirmed us as parents and simply encouraged us to love our daughter even more deeply as we went through this difficult situation together. They emphasized the importance of maintaining good communication and supporting her through the challenging days of pregnancy. We experienced them as God's angels of grace and mercy during a painful time in our lives.

Our daughter is now a single parent attending college and working with teenagers in difficulty. We have a delightful grandson.

That couple recognized our situation of need. They found within themselves the spiritual gifts of compassion and understanding. They shared those gifts with us for our healing. We thank God for giving this couple the gifts of sensitivity, love, and wisdom to minister to us in our time of need.

BIBLE STUDY

In order to help the group experience what this event was like for this woman, invite everyone to read the Bible text over silently first and then to close their eyes while you read the following guided meditation on this story.

Beginning of guided meditation.

Read: Luke 8:40-48 (A Woman Needs Healing)

In a similar way, a woman who had suffered with a painful physical condition for twelve years experienced understanding and healing from Jesus.

Imagine that you are a part of the crowd that meets Jesus at the dock in Capernaum when he returns from the country of the Gerasenes. Imagine Jesus and his disciples getting off the boat. They are immediately surrounded by a crowd of forty to fifty people. Imagine Jairus, a leading citizen of the community, stepping out of the crowd and falling on his knees before Jesus. He weeps as he tells Jesus that his only daughter is sick and dying. He begs Jesus to come to his house and heal her. Imagine Jesus starting off through the crowd following Jairus through the streets of Capernaum to the house where the little girl lay ill.

Now you see a woman who has suffered from hemorrhages for twelve years joining the crowd as it moves through the streets. She's heard about this healer from Nazareth and wonders if he could heal her as well. However, he's on an important mission now and she doesn't want to interrupt him with her need. But on the other hand, if she doesn't see him immediately she may never have another chance. She's already been to dozens of doctors and none of them could help her. Would this healer be any different? Can you imagine the conflict she feels inside?

As she follows Jesus in the crowd, the conviction grows within her that God could heal her through this man. She works her way up in the crowd until she is right behind him. She remembers hearing that God's healing power is even present in the fringe of a holy man's clothes. So she reaches down and touches the fringe of his garment. Immediately she feels the healing power of God move up her arm and throughout her body. She stops in stunned silence realizing that she has been healed. Suddenly, Jesus also stops, looks around and asks, "Who touched me?" Peter explains that many people are in the crowd pressing around him and are touching him. Jesus replies that he knows someone has touched him in faith for he felt God's healing power flowing through him into the life of another.

Imagine the woman stepping out of the crowd trembling with fear and kneeling down before Jesus confessing, "I am the one." Listen to her explain how she had been ill for twelve years, visited many doctors to no avail, and how, when she touched the hem of his garment, she felt God's healing power. See Jesus looking at her with eyes of compassion and love, reaching down and taking her by the hand, and saying to her: "Daughter, it was not touching the robe that healed you. Your faith in God's healing power has made you well. Go with God's peace." Imagine her jumping up, smiling, praising God, and rushing off to tell her family about this good news.

End of guided meditation.

GROUP INTERACTION
Invite the group to divide into pairs and to discuss the questions in the main text.

How did you imagine yourself in the crowd watching this scene? What images or ideas came to mind as you watched this healing take place? What feelings or thoughts did you have during this guided imagination time with Scripture?

DISCUSSION POINT
In what ways are you like the woman with the hemor-rhage?

What kinds of needs might you openly acknowledge?

What kinds of needs might you keep hidden?

Why might you keep needs for healing hidden from others?

DISCUSSION POINT
Why might sharing your needs be risky?

What is the worst thing that could possibly happen were you to share your need for healing?

Sometimes we may be like the woman with the hemorrhage. We don't want to openly acknowledge our needs for healing. We would like to be healed but we want it done privately and don't want anyone else to know. We often present to the world a front that says "everything is just fine with me" when inside we're hurting and longing for healing.

I recently heard a story about two male medical doctors who worked together in surgery for over ten years. They considered themselves friends, saw each other almost every day at work, and sometimes shared family time together socially. However, one of the doctors discovered that he had cancer but he hid that fact from the other doctor for over a year. They worked together, they saw each other regularly, and when the doctor who was ill was asked how he was doing he always said "just fine" even though he was becoming critically ill with cancer. Like that doctor, we often have a hard time acknowledging our needs for healing even to those we might consider our best friends. Like the woman in the Bible text, we often have a hard time openly admitting to God or to anyone else the secret pain and burdens we carry.

In the story, the woman was behind Jesus and only followed him from a distance in the crowd. But when Jesus turned around, she fell on her knees before him and encountered him face to face. She wanted to hide in the crowd but Jesus wanted a face to face encounter with her. In a similar way, we often like to hide in the crowd and simply follow Jesus from a distance. We want to be followers but shy away from opening ourselves up to God in a person-to-person way. However, Christ turns around, calls us to confess openly our need, and then reaches down. He takes us by the hand and says, "My daughter, my son, it is your trusting faith in God's healing power that makes you whole. Live with God's peace in your life." The first step toward experiencing God's healing power in our lives is to openly acknowledge our need for it.

Some of us may need physical healing. Some of us may desire the healing of a loved one. Some of us may need the healing of broken relationships. Some of us may need the healing of painful memories from the past. Whatever our personal need may be, the first step is to openly admit it to Christ. Then we may want to share that need with other Christian friends. And when we take the risk of sharing, we often discover that God has given the gifts necessary for our healing to some of the persons around us.

WRITTEN REFLECTION
Ask group members to follow the instruction in the main text. Then ask them to share as much as feels comfortable with one other person in the group.

DISCUSSION POINT
How might sharing a need for healing open you up to that healing?

In what ways might God present you with persons gifted for your healing?

Write in the space below any personal needs that have come to your mind. What are your desires for healing? What are the pressing concerns in your life right now that you find yourself thinking and brooding over? What situations drain your life energy and keep you from being a whole person?

When we share a need for healing with another person, that very sharing opens us up to the healing that God may be sending through other persons around us. Be aware of the ways in which God may present you with the persons gifted for your healing.

When we think about our life journeys, we remember certain persons who have been there at a particular time of need. We may think about our parents, teachers, pastors, friends, or even strangers who seem to have had the gifts necessary to help us through particularly challenging times in our lives.

Several years ago, I was driving alone late one night on a desolate stretch of road in western South Dakota. I had not seen any other cars on that road for quite some time. Suddenly, my car lost all power and coasted to a stop alongside the road. I got out and looked under the car. There on the ground lay one end of the drive shaft. It was about midnight as I looked around to see if there was any help in sight. About a half mile down the road I saw a farmhouse with the lights still on. I trudged down the road and knocked at the front door. The man who opened the door looked at me and said: "Kent, what are you doing out here this time of night?" To my utter surprise, he was a friend from college days whom I had not seen in ten years and with whom I had lost contact. I explained to him that my car had broken down on the highway near his house. He told me that his Dad owned a gas station in the small town about five miles back and that the mechanic was working late that night. He called the mechanic who came out and towed my car to the station. The mechanic explained that the universal joint had gone out on my car and that they normally didn't have those in stock. He happened to have an extra one on hand, however, and it happened to fit my car. He put it on. Within an hour of my breakdown on a desolate stretch of road, I was back on my way singing praises to God for the numerous positive coincidences that met my need.

I pondered: *What if I had broken down somewhere else? What if my friend had not happened to be up late that night? What if the mechanic hadn't been working late and happened to have the one part I needed?* I had no explanations for any of these questions, only a profound sense of gratitude to God for all of these persons who met my need in the middle of the night.

DISCUSSION POINT

What do you think about the notion of "God-incidences?"

Do you think God causes coincidences to happen?

How do you explain incidences when the coincidences do not happen?

I have a friend who doesn't call events like this coincidences but "God-incidences" because they evoke in us a feeling of praise to God. All of us have experiences like this where we have felt God using the gifts and graces of others to meet our needs.

WRITTEN REFLECTION

Write in the space below the names of persons who have used their gifts to meet your needs and led you to thank God for them.

GROUP INTERACTION
Invite the group to follow the printed instructions.

Share with one other person the names of the persons who have met your needs and evoked a feeling of praise to God within you. Then if you wish, share with the whole group the names of individuals who have been used by God to meet a particular need in your life.

BEFORE NEXT TIME

The leader for next time should ask the pastor or other church leaders if they can add to the leader's list any persons within the church recently or currently in situations causing pain who may need the gifts for ministry of persons in the group.

WORSHIP

BEFORE NEXT TIME

Next time we will begin to look around at the needs of other persons in our congregation. In preparation for that session, make a list of persons you know within your congregation who are going through some experiences of pain in their lives. They might have lost loved ones during the past year or gone through a recent divorce. Or you may make a similar list of relatives, friends, and acquaintances who are undergoing pain in their lives. Come prepared to share your list with others in the group next week.

You may want to conclude your class by reading or singing together "He Touched Me":

Shackled by a heavy burden, neath a load of guilt and shame, then the hand of Jesus touched me, and now I am no longer the same.

Refrain: *He touched me, O He touched me, and O the joy that floods my soul! Something happened, and now I know, He touched me and made me whole.*

Since I met this blessed Savior, since He cleansed and made me whole, I will never cease to praise Him; I'll shout it while eternity rolls.

(Refrain)

(From "He Touched Me" written by William J. Gaither. Copyright © 1963 by William J. Gaither. All rights reserved. Used by permission.)

LIST OF PERSONS IN SITUATIONS OF PAIN
(for next session)

CHAPTER TWO

LOOK AROUND: WHAT DO OTHERS NEED?

WORSHIP

When the group is ready to begin, open with this prayer or one in your own words.

CHECKING IN

If there are new persons in the class today, take a few moments to allow them to introduce themselves and invite the other class members to tell who they are.

Ask also if anyone wishes to share an insight stemming from the last time together. This would also be an appropriate time for persons to share any joys or concerns— including needs for healing.

WRITTEN REFLECTION

GROUP INTERACTION

After allowing time for personal written reflection, go around the group and invite members to mention one of the items on their list. Record the items on the chalkboard or newsprint, if available. Continue to go around the group until all recognized

Begin by praying this prayer:

Our God, we thank you and praise you for the congregation of which we are a part. Open our eyes to see the needs of those around us, open our ears to hear the muffled cries of those in pain, and open our hearts to feel the hurts of others. Help us to look at those around us through your eyes of compassion and love. In Christ's name. Amen.

This session will help you look around at the needs of others in our church community on our way toward discovering our God-given gifts for meeting those needs.

Since the focus of this session is on our local congregation, write in the space below strengths of our congregation. What do you consider to be the strongest aspects of our church's ministry?

strengths have been mentioned. Record each item as spoken without any discussion by the group.

The purpose of this exercise is not to come to a group consensus about your church's strengths. Look instead at the variety of gifts your church already has in place for ministering to the diverse needs of persons.

GROUP INTERACTION

Follow instructions in the main text.

Last session you and other group members were asked to make a list on page 13 of persons who have lost loved ones in our congregation during the past year, who have gone through divorce, or who have experienced some other particular pain in their lives. Share what you discovered.

From the lists of other group members, add any other needs of persons in the congregation. Are there individuals who have lost their jobs or suffered other economic setbacks? Are there persons who struggle to survive natural disasters such as floods or hurricanes? Are there persons who experience alienation from others in their families or in the congregation? Are there persons who are suffering through serious illness in themselves or in someone they love?

DISCUSSION POINT

To what extent is this statement true for you?

<u>Groups often discover that more pain exists right around them than they initially think.</u>

DISCUSSION POINT

Before you worked on your list, to what extent were you aware or oblivious to the pain of people around you in your congregation? Why do you think that was the case?

This is a time to look at the needs of those in our congregation before looking at the gifts you have been given by God to minister to those needs. <u>Sometimes people right around us may be suffering, and we are oblivious to their pain. Spend some time becoming aware of suffering in your congregation.</u>

In a congregation where I once served as pastor, we had a ritual of passing a "friendship pad" down the pew each Sunday morning. Worshipers were asked to write their names and addresses and to indicate any needs to which they would like the church to respond. There were spaces for persons to check if they were members of the church or if they were new to the congregation or if they would like a visit from the pastor.

Every Monday those sheets were collected and processed in our church office by a group of volunteers. They would give me a list of those who were new in the congregation and those who had requested a visit from the pastor. You can imagine my total surprise when our ten-year old son's name showed up on that list one Monday as someone who had requested a visit from the pastor!

DISCUSSION POINT

In what ways might you have overlooked the needs of persons "right under your nose"?

Upon reflection, I realized that I had allowed my schedule to become so full that I had not been spending regular, quality time with our son. He was feeling the pain of having an absent father. When I talked with him later about it, he admitted that his signing the sheet was a way of getting my attention, and it worked! That experience touched me deeply. It became a constant reminder that I must not neglect the needs of my family nor my responsibilities and gifts as a father in the midst of my active involvement in the church.

Your group might want to explore this concern further using the LIFESEARCH *resource on* JUGGLING DEMANDS.

I suspect that I am not alone in this realization. Many of us become so involved in church work and fulfilling all our responsibilities that we overlook and neglect the needs of others that are right under our noses. In fact, work in the church or commitments to our vocations may conflict with our commitments to our families.

BIBLE STUDY

Read: Luke 13:10-17 (Jesus Heals a Bent-Over Woman)

GROUP INTERACTION

Be sure all of the readers are using the same translation of the Bible for this reading. Ask four persons to read these parts: Narrator (all those verses that set the context and are not within quotation marks); Jesus; the Leader of the Synagogue; the Bent-Over Woman.

Position these volunteers in front of the group so that all can experience the high drama and power of this event in the life of a bent-over woman. Invite the person playing the part of the bent-over woman to bend over and

After the reading, spend a few moments in silence reflecting and writing on one of these questions: If you read one of the parts, how did you feel in your particular role? If you did not read one of the parts, with which role did you most identify? Why?

to stay that way until Jesus lays his hands on her and heals her. Read it over a second time with a bent-over man to convey the point that all of us, women and men, are often bent-over by the burdens of life and need the healing power of Christ.

DISCUSSION POINT

Try allowing five to ten minutes for women only to share, then five to ten minutes for men only to summarize what they heard and to respond.

Luke 13:11 says that a "spirit" caused the woman to be bent over. Luke 13:16 identifies the spirit that bound her as Satan. What are the evil spirits and attitudes that cause women to feel bound and burdened today? Many women experience sexism as an evil spirit or attitude in our society that burdens their lives. Are you aware of ways in which women are treated unfairly in your church or community? Do women have the same opportunities as men to develop and use their God-given gifts in our world today? These questions provide a good opportunity for the women in the group to share and for the men to listen carefully.

DISCUSSION POINT

What are the burdens and experiences of life that cause men to be bent over today?

How are men pressured to succeed in your community? in your church?

In what ways are men prevented from expressing their pain?

GROUP INTERACTION

Allow five to ten minutes for men only to share, then five to ten minutes for women only to summarize what they heard and to respond.

While women are sometimes burdened by a society that treats them as "sex-objects," men are sometimes burdened by a society that treats them as "success-objects." Men may feel absolutely worthless and of no value if they are not considered successful in their chosen field. Men are often burdened by the idea that "real men don't cry" and that they are not allowed to feel or to express emotion even when they're in pain. These observations provide a good opportunity for the men in the group to share the burdens they carry as men and for the women to listen carefully.

The woman in the story had been bent over for eighteen years. Evidently, she regularly attended synagogue worship and everyone was used to seeing her bent over. Perhaps they had gotten used to seeing her in this condition and no longer empathized with her pain. But the text tells us that when Jesus saw her he called her over to him, laid his healing hands on her back, and spoke the words of healing; then she stood up straight and began praising God. Jesus didn't look through

DISCUSSION POINT

Who are the women and men in your congregation who carry long-time burdens?

In what ways have you "gotten used" to them?

DISCUSSION POINT

Of what circumstances are you aware in which someone has found in their own pain some gifts with which they could help someone else?

her or past her but at her with eyes of compassion and responded in healing ways. <u>Who are the people in your congregation who need you to look at them through the eyes of Jesus, feel their pain, and respond in healing ways?</u>

People who are suffering because of the death of a spouse, parent, child, relative, or friend are present in every congregation. In the congregation I serve, we brought some of those persons together so that they might support and comfort one another in walking through the valley of the shadow of death. Consequently, our church began a Grief Support Group where those who had lost loved ones could gather each week for prayer, encouragement, and support. Sometimes they read books dealing with grief or watch and discuss videos on grief. But always personal sharing and prayer takes place.

The word spread throughout the community that such a group was available. Persons from other congregations and some who had no church home began to attend. One participant was a man who had lost his wife to cancer and was raising three boys. He was working through his grief quite effectively but he hurt for his sons. They had never wept over her death, nor could they seem to find a way to express their pain over the loss of their mother. He suspected they did not want to share their grief with him for fear of burdening him further. Neither would they go for counseling. So he suggested that our congregation also begin a grief group for teenagers since several persons in his group had teenagers who had lost a mother or father.

About eight to ten teenagers began to meet with a sensitive advisor in a separate room at the same time their parents met. At one of those meetings, all three of the man's teenage sons wept openly as they shared with other teenagers about the loss of their mother. For the first time they cried over her death. They experienced their tears as healing. A family that had been bent over with grief began to find healing and hope. Furthermore, persons who had been through their own grief discovered that they had received the spiritual gifts necessary for helping heal others in grief and leading them to God through a time of sorrow.

The congregation developed a similar ministry with those who had been through divorce. We discovered that persons who go through divorce often feel alienated and unwelcome in their congregation. At the time they need the warmth and understanding of Christian friends most, they often feel it the least. Consequently, we sent a woman who had been through divorce to a training program for leading divorce recovery groups. She has now led five ten-week classes. In those classes divorced persons from our congregation and from the community have come to new life by learning and sharing about their experiences.

When we look around in our congregations with the compassionate eyes of Christ, we see persons who have been bent over by serious illness in their families, the loss of jobs or other economic crises in their lives, alienation in their families, disappointment in the achievement of their life goals, or other painful circumstances in life. Many churches have a number of persons who have a limited ability to leave home and who may be lonely or need regular contact from caring persons in the church. The first step in discovering our spiritual gifts is to look at the needs right around us. Then we might pray for Christ's healing presence and look for the gifts God has given us for those ministries.

WRITTEN REFLECTION

Write in the space below the names of persons in your congregation who are carrying particularly heavy burdens.

DISCUSSION POINT

How much ministering to needs is done by your pastor and how much by other persons in your church?

What do you think of the statement that both pastors and lay persons are called to the ministry of caring for the needs of others?

<u>How is your congregation responding to those needs? Note that the question is "what is your *congregation* doing?" not "what is your *pastor* doing?" to care for persons in need.</u> Sometimes congregations feel that they have hired the pastor to do the ministry of caring in a church and therefore the lay persons are exempted from that responsibility. Sometimes the pastor assumes that responsibility alone and does not allow lay persons to use their gifts of ministry. However, the New Testament makes no such distinction. All Christians—pastors and lay persons alike—are called to the ministry of caring for the needs of others in a local congregation.

Next time we will look beyond the needs of persons in our congregation to the needs of persons in our community and world. To prepare, visit a homeless shelter, food pantry, or other places in your community that care for the poor. Find out how many people they serve and how they are supported. Visit with homeless persons and listen sensitively to their life journeys and their pain. You might be able to visit a jail or

BEFORE NEXT TIME

You can either arrange for your group to do one or more of these visits together, or you can have individuals do them on their own.

WORSHIP

BEFORE NEXT TIME

prison to discover how persons in that situation are being cared for. You might also want to visit with your pastor or other church leaders about how emergency needs are cared for in your church and community.

Come prepared next week to share what you've discovered about needs in your community.

To conclude this session on looking around at the needs of persons in your congregation, sing or read "We Are the Church." .

Chorus: I am the church! You are the church! We are the church together! All who follow Jesus, all around the world! Yes, we're the church together!

The church is not a building, the church is not a steeple, the church is not a resting place, the church is a people. (chorus)

We're many kinds of people, with many kinds of faces, all colors and all ages, too, from all times and places. (chorus)

Sometimes the church is marching, sometimes it's bravely burning, sometimes it's riding, sometimes hiding, always it's learning. (chorus)

And when the people gather, there's singing and there's praying, there's laughing and there's crying sometimes, all of it saying: (chorus)

At Pentecost some people received the Holy Spirit and told the Good News through the world to all who would hear it. (chorus)

REFLECTIONS ON VISITING PERSONS IN NEED (for next session)

CHAPTER THREE

LOOK BEYOND: WHAT DOES THE WORLD NEED NOW?

WORSHIP

Begin by praying this prayer:

O God of all people and places, we thank you for the marvelous diversity that you have created and placed in this world. We praise you for loving the world so much that you sent your Son to be the light of this world. Inspire us to allow your loving light to shine in us and through us that the world might be transformed. In Christ's name. Amen.

CHECKING IN

Begin this session by welcoming any new persons to the group. Invite anyone to share significant events that may have occurred in their life since last time.

This time you will be looking beyond yourselves and the needs of persons in your congregation to the needs of persons in the world. Last time you were encouraged to visit a homeless shelter or community food pantry in your community or area. Or you may have visited a jail or talked with someone who works with the poor. These visits were intended to open your eyes to the needs of people in your area as you begin to reflect on how God wants to use your gifts for the transformation of the world into a community of justice and love.

DISCUSSION POINT

Debrief the members of the group on their visits using these questions and/or other questions as appropriate.

Spend some time reflecting on your visit to a shelter or food pantry. How many people does the shelter or pantry serve each month? Where do they get their resources? Where do they get their volunteers? Did you meet any of the clients of the shelter or pantry? How did you feel about being in such a setting? Does anyone in your group volunteer in ministries to the poor? What assistance does your church provide to the agencies that serve the poor? Has your church considered providing food or lodging for the poor? How does your congregation respond to emergency needs in your community? Who ministers to the needs of persons in jail or prison in your community? Has anyone in your congregation or community been on a short-term work-camp in this country or abroad? Has your community or area experienced a natural disaster such as a flood, earthquake, or hurricane? How did the church respond in that crisis? Are there any missionaries in your congregation or community who might reflect with you on the broader needs of our world? Please use these questions as a way to focus your attention on the needs of people beyond your own congregation.

If the group identifies such a missionary and wishes to do so, invite him or her to an extra session of your group to help members reflect about the needs around them.

On June 9, 1972, a devastating flash flood ripped through Rapid City, South Dakota. About fourteen inches of rain fell in two hours, collected in the Black Hills, and became a roaring flood through this community of 50,000 people. The flood caused the Canyon Lake Dam to break, sending a wall of water fifteen to twenty feet high through the heart of the city. In just a couple of hours, about a thousand homes and another thousand mobile homes were destroyed. More than two hundred persons lost their lives and many others were injured. I became a volunteer pastor to help in flood recovery efforts and shortly thereafter became a pastor of the congregation hardest hit by the flood.

The churches of the community pooled their own resources as well as resources received from their national denominations to assist families in recovering from this devastating disaster. The United Methodist Committee on Relief responded with funds and personnel and helped to coordinate other church responses. The Mennonite Central Committee sent a large number of skilled volunteer carpenters who helped persons throughout the community clean, rebuild, and repair hundreds of damaged homes. Government agencies set up mobile home parks throughout the community to provide temporary housing for persons who had lost everything.

The emotional toll was even greater than the physical loss. About two months after the flood, an elderly gentlemen in our congregation who had lost both his home and his wife of more than fifty years in the flood took his own life. Nine members of the congregation I served were killed in the flood. The body of one of the children was never found. One teenage girl in our congregation went every day for weeks to the concrete slab on which her home had sat and wept because every physical thing that she had ever possessed was gone.

Nonetheless, out of this terrible experience, the people of the community began to experience new life. For the first time, all denominational barriers fell. The churches of the community worked together to help everyone in the community whether they were a part of a congregation or not. Mennonites were housed in a Catholic school and worked side by side with priests and nuns. Native Americans and Caucasians who had never spoken with one another became close friends as they worked together to rebuild the community. The flood was no respecter of persons and had destroyed lives and homes in the wealthiest and the poorest sections of the city. This crisis brought out the best in people in terms of generosity and compassion for those in need.

Living through such a crisis also helped people become more

clear about lasting values in life. One woman in our church had a collection of antiques from all over the world of which she was very proud. She and her husband had lost their home and all of her antiques, but they both survived. After the flood, she shared with me that this terrible experience had helped her see that the most valuable thing in life was her faith in God and her relationships with those she loved. Those values could not be destroyed by a flood. She realized she had placed too much value on physical things that could be taken away rather than relationships with God and loved ones which endure forever.

Another woman who lost her husband in the flood began calling on people in the church in times of grief or crisis. She found fulfillment in transforming her own life experience into a means of ministry.

DISCUSSION POINT

In what ways do you think this statement is accurate or inaccurate?

Even out of this experience persons of faith discovered how God brings new life and hope. Persons and communities regularly experience the floods and storms of life that beat them down. <u>We look to God to call forth the gifts necessary to minister in these times of critical need.</u>

DISCUSSION POINT

Discuss crises in your community and how the Christian churches respond to those needs.

In recent years, floods, hurricanes, tornados, drought, and riots have caused severe suffering in many parts of the world. <u>Reflect on the nearby disasters of which you are aware and how God has raised up and gifted persons to minister in those situations.</u>

BIBLE STUDY

Read: Luke 10:25-37 (The Parable of the Wounded Man)

This parable told by Jesus is usually called the parable of the good Samaritan. It focuses on the compassionate Samaritan who assisted a man beaten by robbers and left half-dead alongside the road between Jerusalem and Jericho. I'm calling it the parable of the wounded man because I want us to look at the story from his point of view.

GROUP INTERACTION

Ask persons to read and act out the following parts: Narrator; the Lawyer; Jesus; the Beaten Man; two or three Robbers; the Priest; the Levite; the Samaritan; and the Innkeeper. The person reading Jesus' part should read the story with pauses to enable the actors to act out his words. Use the same translation of the New Testament for this reading.

Youth in our confirmation classes always enjoy acting out this story. They become enthusiastic about who gets to play the part of the robbers and beat up on a classmate. More than once we've had to restrain overeager robbers. However, I trust that will not be a problem with adults as you reenact this text in order to experience the dramatic power and moral impact of Jesus' story.

WRITTEN REFLECTION

Ask persons to reflect individually on the six questions in the main text. Then ask them to share their reflections in small groups of three or four and/or with the whole group.

After the dramatic reading of this story, write out your reflections to the following questions:

1. Why do you think Jesus told a story rather than giving a direct answer to the lawyer's "who is my neighbor" question?

2. Why do you think the Jewish religious leaders (the priest from the Temple in Jerusalem and the Levite, the designated lay leader of the Temple) ignored the needs of the wounded man and passed by on the other side of the road? Read Leviticus 21:1-3 and Numbers 19:11-22 to gain insight about their fear of touching a dead body.

3. Why did the Samaritan, a member of a group hated by Jews, stop to help a wounded Jewish man?

4. How do you think the wounded man felt as he saw two Jewish religious leaders pass him by? How do you think he felt when a Samaritan nursed his wounds, took him to safety, and paid for his continuing care?

5. Who are the wounded persons in our society? In what ways does the church ignore their needs or give time and resources to minister to them?

6. Who would you nominate for the "Good Samaritan Award" in your church or community and why?

During the past few years, I've led several groups through *Disciple: Becoming Disciples Through Bible Study* (Cokesbury, 1993). As part of our study of the Gospel of Luke, we visited a shelter for homeless persons. We went to the Union Gospel Mission in our community on a night when I was to lead the worship service there. About forty homeless persons arrived for the service, which would be followed by a free meal and overnight accommodations.

During the worship service, a man in our *Disciple* group saw a man with whom he had once worked. About six years earlier, both men had held good jobs with a trucking firm. They had often worked together. However, the trucking firm went out of business. One of the men went on to find a job with another firm but the other man could not find adequate employment. After visiting with his friend for awhile, the man in the *Disciple* group shared with me, "There but for the grace of God go I." He realized that if he had not found another job, he could be in the same circumstance as his friend.

DISCUSSION POINT

What do you think about this observation?

What circumstances might you be in "but for the grace of God?"

This experience had a profound impact on the man from our church and his wife. They began to provide generous financial support to the shelter and became weekly volunteers there. They invited me to join them one Friday night as they fixed a meal at the shelter. I witnessed the love and compassion with which they served that meal to persons in need. Discovering the genuine needs of homeless persons, they also found within themselves the gifts and the desire to serve God and others in this ministry.

DISCUSSION POINT

What other examples can you give of this dynamic at work?

DISCUSSION POINT

What spiritual gifts can you begin to see in yourself in response to the needs of others?

How do you feel about looking for your spiritual gifts in response to the needs of those around you?

Our world is filled with the needs of people who feel beaten and wounded alongside the road of life. Will we as religious persons today pass by on the other side? Or will we identify with the pain of suffering persons and share our time and resources in healing ways? Becoming sensitive to the needs of persons in the world will help to clarify our spiritual gifts and will evoke within us a desire to use them for the transformation of the world.

BEFORE NEXT TIME

Next time we will look within ourselves to discover the gifts God has placed there for ministry in our church and in our community. In preparation, make a list of the types of experiences that you most enjoy, and make a second list of the things in the church and world that most upset you.

WORSHIP

In closing you may want to sing or read "Let There Be Peace on Earth":

Let there be peace on earth, and let it begin with me; let there be peace on earth, the peace that was meant to be.* With God our creator, children all are we. Let us walk with each other in perfect harmony. Let peace begin with me; let this be the moment now. With every step I take, let this be my solemn vow: to take each moment and live each moment in peace eternally. Let there be peace on earth, and let it begin with me.

* Original words: With God as our Father, brothers all are we. Let me walk with my brother in perfect harmony.

(From "Let There Be Peace on Earth," by Sy Miller and Jill Jackson. Copyright © 1955 by Sy Miller and Jill Jackson. Assigned 1955 to Jan-Lee Music. Copyright © 1956 by Jan-Lee Music. International copyright secured. Used by permission.)

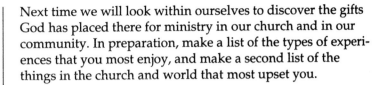

BEFORE NEXT TIME

TYPES OF EXPERIENCES I MOST ENJOY

THINGS IN THE CHURCH AND WORLD THAT MOST UPSET ME

CHAPTER FOUR

EXPLORE WITHIN: WHAT ARE MY GIFTS?

WORSHIP

CHECKING IN

Invite members of the group to share the highlights in their lives since your group last met. Give them a moment to remember what has happened in their lives since then and encourage them to share briefly one of the most significant events. If there are persons in the group who have suffered tragedies recently, take time to offer prayer, either silent or spoken, for them and their situation. Also take time to offer prayers of thanksgiving for any particular blessings that are shared.

Begin by praying this prayer:

O God of the depths, thank you for placing your gifts deep within my heart. Lead me to the treasures you have buried in my life, celebrate with me when they are discovered, and empower me to use them in your ministry for the transformation of the world. In Christ's name. Amen.

During the past three sessions you have been looking at the needs of persons in your congregation and your world for the healing and hope offered through Jesus Christ. Now you will begin to explore within yourselves individually as well as within your group the spiritual gifts God has placed there to meet those identified needs.

In a congregation I once served as pastor, there was a retired, single, school teacher who became upset if she was not visited regularly by her pastor. If she did not receive a pastoral visit every month or so she would begin to complain at committee meetings and to her friends in the church that the pastor was not doing enough home calling. When I heard of the concerns, I would generally make an appointment to stop by to see her, We would have refreshments and a pleasant visit, and she would be delighted that her pastor had come to see her. She had no relatives around, and I began to realize that she was simply lonely for someone with whom to visit. Asking the pastor to come to visit was her way of dealing with her loneliness.

One day as I was brooding about this, another way of dealing with her loneliness occurred to me. I called her on the phone and invited her to go with me to visit another woman in our congregation. This other woman had arthritis so severe that she had a limited ability to leave home and needed help to get around. Going on the visit with me, the retired teacher experienced firsthand the depths of this woman's need for love, care, and assistance in order to survive on her own.

In the course of our conversation, we learned that the woman with a limited ability to leave home needed someone to help her with her shopping, to take her to her doctor's appointments, and generally to be her friend. My teacher friend was shocked that she had no one to take care of these basic needs. So she volunteered to stop by at least once or twice a week to assist her newfound friend. Later I shared with my teacher friend about another person who needed some regular visits and she agreed to visit that person as well. She became so involved in caring for the needs of others that she was not lonely anymore. She found herself in regular contact with persons who needed her love and concern. From that time on she never again complained about not having a pastoral visit: she was doing pastoral visits herself and finding a fulfilling ministry in the process. She discovered her gift for caring for others in God's name, and she was a wonderful blessing in many homes.

DISCUSSION POINT

What do you think about these claims?

What began as this woman's complaint was discovered to be her passion and gift for ministry. One way we discover our gifts for ministry is by considering the areas we complain about most often. Our complaints may simply be the dark side of our passions.

DISCUSSION POINT

What do you think of the notion that God prods you to ministry through your complaints?

If you find yourself complaining about the quality of worship in your church, God may be calling you to volunteer to assist the pastor and other worship leaders in planning and leading vital, creative, meaningful worship services. If you find yourself complaining about the level of stewardship in your congregation, God may be calling you to tithe and to inspire others to that kind of financial commitment. If you find yourself complaining that your congregation is not doing enough for missions, God may be calling you to organize a mission workteam or to help educate the congregation about the needs of people beyond your local church. If you have complaints about the educational program, or the homeless people in your community, or the care persons with a limited ability to leave home receive, then God may be calling you through your complaints to begin ministry in those settings. If you know what your complaint is about the church, then you have a pretty good idea about where God is prodding you to use your gifts in ministry.

WRITTEN REFLECTION

In preparation for this session you were asked to list the things that upset you most in the church or in society. Look again at that list on page 27. In the space below list two or three of the areas about which you find yourself complaining most.

GROUP INTERACTION

Divide the group into smaller groups of three or four persons. Allow ample time for the smaller groups to help each of their members explore areas of strong complaints and possible related gifts.

You may find yourself resisting this exercise. Often the stronger your resistance, then the more clarity you may discover about your gifts for ministry. Allow others to help you discover your ministry gift on the other side of your most persistent complaint.

BIBLE STUDY

Read: Mark 1:16-20 (The Calling of Four Fishermen)

In order to experience this text in a contemporary setting, first read this text silently. Then write in the space below your contemporary paraphrase of this event.

WRITTEN REFLECTION

A paraphrase is intended to convey the essential meaning of the text by using contemporary words and images. For example, rather than saying Jesus passed along the Sea of Galilee, you might choose a local body of water. Or you might not choose a body of water at all but a local shopping mall or other location where people might be found at work. Rather than calling fishermen to fish for people, you might imagine calling farmers to cultivate spiritual growth among people or bankers to invest in disadvantaged people or nurses to inject people with God's love. Don't allow these suggestions to limit your own creativity. Just imagine Jesus coming to call persons

GROUP INTERACTION

After group members have completed their paraphrases, ask them to share in groups of three or four and/or with the whole group.

in some contemporary setting. Then use your own words and images to convey how Jesus might call persons to use the gifts they already have for fulfilling his ministry today.

Sometimes those who write about spiritual gifts make a great distinction between natural gifts, abilities, and skills on the one hand and the gifts of the spirit on the other. They maintain that spiritual gifts are radically different from one's natural gifts and abilities.

However, in the text that you just studied from Mark's Gospel, Jesus builds on the natural gifts and skills of Peter, Andrew, James, and John. He transforms those gifts for use in leading people into the kingdom of God. They will now use skills formerly used in reaching out to bring fish into their boats instead to reach out to bring persons into Christ's presence. This means that Christ can transform and use any skill or ability that we have in order to glorify God and to bring people into a vital relationship with Christ.

Furthermore, all of our natural gifts and abilities are gifts from God in the first place. We can choose either of two options for using those gifts. We can use those gifts for merely selfish purposes; or we can dedicate them to the glory of God for use in building up the body of Christ for the common

DISCUSSION POINT

What do you think of this understanding of "spiritual gifts?"

What other examples can you think of in which natural gifts might be used to lead persons spiritually to God?

DISCUSSION POINT

Keep this discussion brief. Another opportunity will be offered later to explore this way of discernment in greater depth.

good. For example, one person may be given a beautiful voice for singing. They can use that voice for merely selfish purposes to make themselves famous; or they can dedicate that gift to the glory of God and use it to lead others to faith in Christ. <u>A spiritual gift may be a natural gift that is used to lead persons spiritually to God.</u>

You can also discern the gifts of the spirit that God has placed within you by considering what it is that brings joy and excitement into your life. Sometimes, Christians think that the spiritual must be serious. They appear to believe that if something brings joy and excitement into your life, it must not be of God. However, Jesus said, "I came that they may have life, and have it abundantly" (John 10:10). <u>What are the aspects and activities of your life that enable you to experience joyful, abundant life?</u>

One member of our congregation is an avid fisherman. In the summertime he fishes on lakes and rivers; in the wintertime he goes ice fishing. Fishing is the love and passion of his life. One summer he discovered that many children in our community had never been fishing. He thought that was terrible, so he organized a free fishing derby at a nearby lake and provided all the equipment, bait, and transportation for any child who wanted to go fishing. He recruited some of his fishing friends to assist him. Together they provided an exciting opportunity for children to get the thrill of catching their first fish.

At first I was a little skeptical about the value of this experience. But then I saw numerous little girls and boys who had no father in their homes being affirmed, encouraged, and cared for by these rugged fishermen. I sensed the love of Christ reaching out to those children, many of whom felt abandoned by the men in their lives. I realized that God can use even the gifts and enthusiasm for fishing to spread God's love to hurting children.

WRITTEN REFLECTION

GROUP INTERACTION

Ask persons to share their responses in groups of three or four.

BEFORE NEXT TIME

WORSHIP

In the space below write out some of your activities that bring joy and excitement to your life. Ponder how these activities can be surrendered to God in such a way that God can use them in ministry to the needs of persons. Think about the needs you have discussed in the previous three sessions to determine where your interests and enthusiasm intersect with those needs.

In preparation for next time, make a list of all of the members of your group. Then write down what you perceive to be some of each member's gifts and abilities for ministry. (See next page.) It's important that you do this in advance since it will be a major part of the next session.

Conclude this session by singing or reading "Open My Eyes, That I May See":

Open my eyes, that I may see glimpses of truth thou hast for me; place in my hands the wonderful key that shall unclasp and set me free.

Refrain:
Silently now I wait for thee, ready, my God, thy will to see. (Open my eyes) (Open my ears) (Open my heart), illumine me, Spirit divine!

Open my ears, that I may hear voices of truth thou sendest clear; and while the wavenotes fall on my ear, everything false will disappear. (chorus)

Open my mouth, and let me bear gladly the warm truth everywhere; open my heart and let me prepare love with thy children thus to share. (chorus)

(From "Open My Eyes, That I May See," by Clara H. Scott.)

GROUP MEMBERS	GIFTS FOR MINISTRY
_____	_____
_____	_____
_____	_____
_____	_____
_____	_____
_____	_____
_____	_____
_____	_____
_____	_____
_____	_____
_____	_____
_____	_____
_____	_____
_____	_____
_____	_____
_____	_____

CHAPTER FIVE

EXPLORE AROUND: WHAT ARE YOUR GIFTS?

WORSHIP

CHECKING IN

Invite the group to share any reflections on what has come to them during this past week. Also be sure to check on whether anyone has any joys or concerns to share with the group.

DISCUSSION POINT

Begin by praying this prayer:

O God, who has called us into this group to deepen our faith and expand our growth, we thank you for every person here. Thank you for your light which shines through each person's eyes and for your words spoken through each one's voice. May we see the gifts you have placed in each individual and call them forth to bring glory to you and to serve the needs of people everywhere. In Christ's name. Amen.

Last time you explored your complaints and your desires as areas for the discovery of your spiritual gifts. <u>Have you caught yourself complaining about something and then wondering if that is just the dark side of one of your passions? Is your complaint an indication of where you are called to ministry? Have you surrendered the activities that you enjoy most into God's hands to be transformed into areas of ministry?</u>

None of us can see ourselves objectively. Because we can only look at ourselves through our own eyes and experiences, we have only one point of view to assess our gifts and graces. Our own assessment of ourselves, while critically important, is nevertheless incomplete. That is one reason why God places us in a community of believers.

Others often see in us gifts that we fail to observe. Their recognition of those gifts may encourage us to acknowledge and develop gifts otherwise left undiscovered. Consequently, the purpose of this session is to allow the group to share their perceptions of each person's gifts in order to acknowledge, affirm, and use gifts that might have gone unrecognized and unused in God's work.

DISCUSSION POINT

In what ways do you see yourself in these descriptions?

Sometimes persons pretend not to recognize their own gifts because they're afraid of appearing arrogant. They fear that others will laugh at them. Or they are uncertain of themselves. Many of us suspect that we have certain gifts within us. However, until someone else recognizes and affirms those gifts, we sometimes refuse to acknowledge them or use them in the service of the church and the world. Furthermore, we sometimes refuse to recognize gifts within ourselves because we do not want to accept the responsibility nor risk using that gift to the glory of God and the service of others. To say that we have no gifts or to refuse to recognize our gifts is a safer approach. It allows us to hide our talents and gives us an excuse for withdrawing from the ministries to which God calls us.

In a Bible study program of which I was a part, we had a session in which we helped identify one another's gifts. One young woman in the group was very conscientious in her preparation for each class. She read her lesson in advance, filled out her workbook regularly, and often did extra research on the topic under discussion. However, she was very shy and did not share as much as many other members of the group.

When we came to the session on identifying one another's gifts, many in the group identified her as a future teacher for an adult Bible study class. When that happened, she broke down in tears. She had secretly longed to do exactly that but felt that because she was not as talkative as many others in the group, no one would see her as a teacher. Persons in your group might secretly believe they have certain gifts for ministry, but will never develop and use those gifts unless someone else affirms and confirms that gift in them.

WRITTEN REFLECTION

In the space below you are invited to list some of your gifts that you pretend not to be aware of. You'll not be asked to share this list with anyone else. However, later—after others have affirmed the gifts they see in you—you may want to compare what you have written here and what they said.

DISCUSSION POINT

As the text indicates, do not ask persons to share their lists. However, you might ask if anyone wishes to share how they felt about doing this written reflection.

Several years ago, the congregation where I served as pastor invited a clergyman from Australia to lead a week of special worship services in our parish. When he arrived, he informed me that God had given him the gift of healing and that he would like to conduct healing services in the church. This was not exactly what we expected, but we wanted to be open to wherever God was leading. So we affirmed his desire. For the first time persons in that parish intensely focused on prayers for physical healing, spiritual healing, emotional healing, the healing of broken relationships, and the healing of painful memories. To the surprise of many, we witnessed the healing of numerous persons in a variety of ways.

For many persons, this kind of healing will prove controversial. In the interest of spending most of your time on persons' spiritual gifts as such, do not let your group become sidetracked into a discussion of immediate physical healing.

Our Australian friend helped us to see that when we pray for healing, God may heal immediately; or God may heal gradually; or God may not heal at all in the way we expected, but give the healing grace necessary to live victoriously with the situation. On a few occasions, persons asked for healing prayer and were healed immediately. On one occasion, we went to the home of a man who had back pain so severe that he could not get out of his chair without help. We laid hands on him, thanked God for his healing, and then waited in silence as tears rolled down the man's cheeks. After about five minutes, he got up out of the chair without help and declared "the pain's gone." Later he came by the church to thank God for his healing and to tell me that he felt so good, he was going to help his son re-roof his house! Sometimes God heals immediately.

Sometimes God heals gradually through the care of compassionate and competent medical personnel. One woman we prayed for had lost sight in one eye due to a diabetic condition. She had been told by specialists that she would eventually lose sight in the other eye. She prepared herself for total blindness by practicing making the bed and cleaning the house while blindfolded. She had a condition in her good eye where there were "floaters"—weakened blood vessels— that needed to be treated monthly lest one break and cause immediate blindness. After healing prayer, her doctor was surprised to find fewer and fewer floaters until finally there were none. The prospect of losing sight in that eye became drastically reduced. Now, fifteen years later, she is still able to see out of an eye that was supposed to go blind years ago. Sometimes God heals gradually.

And sometimes God gives us the grace to live victoriously with the situation. The apostle Paul was not healed from his "thorn in the flesh" but rather discovered Christ's grace to be sufficient for his life (2 Corinthians 12:7-9). A woman with a severe case of arthritis came forward one night for healing prayer. After the service, she was proclaiming what a wonderful service it was and how great God is. I asked, "Is your arthritis better?" She paused and said, "Oh, no, it still hurts as much as ever; but isn't God wonderful!" It was as if she was given the grace to live above her disease and to praise God anyway.

During the course of the week, our Australian friend identified several persons in our congregation, including myself, who had the gift of healing but were afraid to use it. I had many prejudices against persons who identified themselves as healers, and I certainly didn't want to be classified with them. However, with the understanding that I would be more intentional in lifting people up to God for healing but that it was always God's decision about how God would respond, I found myself affirming a gift for healing prayer.

In the past I had always prayed for sick people, but I admit that I didn't expect much to happen as a result of that prayer. When I was able to acknowledge a gift for healing prayer, that acknowledgment changed my attitude. God was able to use me in healing ways.

God has given all of us numerous gifts for expressing God's love for others. When we refuse to acknowledge the gift, we limit God's ability to use us in carrying out Christian ministry in the world. Sometimes, we simply need someone else to recognize a gift in us so that we can affirm it and allow God to use it for the transformation of the world.

BIBLE STUDY

Ask the group to follow the instructions in the main text.

Read: Matthew 9:35-10:4 (Jesus Empowers Disciples)
To study this text try using what is called the theological approach to Bible study (*Teaching the Bible to Adults and Youth*, by Dick Murray; Abingdon, 1987). Read this text through three times silently, with reflection time in between. The first time you read it, ask yourself these questions: What does this passage tell us about God? What do you see implied about the nature of God as you read these verses? What is the image of God revealed through the activities and words of Jesus in this passage? Write out your response in the space below.

The second time you read this passage through silently, ask yourself these questions: What does this passage tell us about people? What are the characteristics of human beings implied in this text? What does it reveal about the human condition? Write your answer in the space below:

The third time you read this passage, ask yourself these questions: What does this passage tell us about the relationship between God and human beings? From the point of view of this text, what is implied about how God relates to people? Write your answer in the space below:

DISCUSSION POINT

Ask members to share their responses with the whole group.

DISCUSSION POINT

What would you add to or change in this summary statement of Matthew 9:35–10:4?

Jesus felt the deep needs of the crowds, had compassion on them, and then asked God to empower and send out persons to meet the needs of the people—the need for healing and to hear the good news of the Kingdom. Jesus then called twelve of his followers, gave them the gifts for healing and proclamation, and sent them out to use those gifts for the transformation of the world.

The Twelve whom Jesus chose appear to be very ordinary persons. They had no wealth, academic background, social position, or exceptional talents. They were fishermen, tax collectors, probably farmers, and at least one revolutionary zealot. When Jesus told them that they had the gifts to heal people and proclaim the presence of God's kingdom, they may have resisted the idea at first. They probably did not believe that they had such gifts. However they went anyway and discovered that God could use them to change the course of history. Jesus looks at us, who may seem rather ordinary, and sees the potential gifts for transforming the church and the world into the kingdom of God on earth.

WRITTEN REFLECTION

In the space below, write the names of each person in your group. Lift each person up to God in prayer privately, and then write out what you perceive to be her or his gifts. You may see in different persons gifts for teaching, preaching, healing, visiting, administrating, showing compassion, listening, encouraging, visioning, leading, inspiring, enduring, caring, facilitating, praying, singing, believing, hoping, loving, empowering, or any one of many other qualities that God needs to make people whole. Write down whatever comes to mind as you think of each person.

GROUP INTERACTION

This interaction is the climax of this session and should not be rushed. Help group members understand that they are to receive the comments of the other group members without discounting those comments or arguing. Questions for clarification are permitted.

Now focus on one person at a time as each of the other members of the group share one or more gifts he or she sees in that individual. When your turn comes, simply write down what is said without discounting any of the gifts mentioned by others in the group. This is a sacred time, for God is seeking to use these moments for the transformation of persons and the world.

BEFORE NEXT TIME

In preparation for next time read 1 Corinthians 12 and 13 as if you were reading this passage for the first time.

WORSHIP

Conclude by singing or reading together "Pass It On":

It only takes a spark to get a fire going, and soon all those around can warm up in its glowing. That's how it is with God's love once you've experienced it; you spread his love to everyone; you want to pass it on.

What a wondrous time is spring, when all the trees are budding; the birds begin to sing, the flowers start their blooming. That's how it is with God's love once you've experienced it; you want to sing, it's fresh like spring, you want to pass it on.

I wish for you, my friend, this happiness that I've found; you can depend on him, it matters not where you're bound. I'll shout it from the mountaintop; I want my world to know; the Lord of love has come to me, I want to pass it on.

BEFORE NEXT TIME

REFLECTIONS ON 1 CORINTHIANS 12 AND 13

CHAPTER SIX

EXPLORE BEYOND: WHERE NEEDS AND GIFTS INTERSECT

WORSHIP

CHECKING IN

Be sure to allow time for persons to share their joys and concerns.

Group members will have had time since last session to digest the group's assessment of their spiritual gifts. Allow time now to let persons debrief that assessment using the question in the text.

DISCUSSION POINT

What do you think about this statement?

Begin by praying this prayer:

O God, we thank you for placing us in this context of life where our gifts are needed. We know that you are eager for us to get on with it and commit ourselves totally to you and the work you seek to accomplish through us. Lead us today, Lord, that we may "know thee more clearly, love thee more dearly, and follow thee more nearly." In Christ's name. Amen.

(Quoted part from Richard of Chichester, England, 13th cent.)

At the end of last session, you were asked to write down the gifts and graces that others observe in you. Some people may have been surprised at some of the gifts others thought they had. Some people may have been surprised that other class members did not identify gifts they themselves felt they possessed. Share any surprises you felt as a result of listening to other persons assess your gifts. How closely does your assessment of your own gifts match with the observations from other persons?

This last session will help you explore the places where your gifts intersect with the needs of persons in the church and in the world around you. It will also invite you to commit yourself to those areas of ministry. Persons who may be deeply concerned about the needs of others but are not in touch with the power of God often burn out or become cynical in their attempt to meet the needs of people on their own strengths. And those persons who may be in touch with God but are not sensitive to the needs of others often find themselves ineffective in making a positive difference in the world. Faithfulness and effectiveness result when we become aware of God's gifts within us and then offer those gifts in ministry to the needs of persons around us.

In the introduction to this study book, I suggested that we find God's will for our lives when we discover the places where the needs of the world and our God-given gifts inter-

DISCUSSION POINT

sect. A colleague of mine puts it this way: "We are called to be where the desires of our heart and the hungers of the world meet." Throughout this study we have been considering some of the places where people in the world are in pain and need God's healing touch. We have also brooded over the treasures and gifts God placed in us. Now, at this time, do you have any feeling about where those two dynamics intersect?

DISCUSSION POINT

What do you understand by "commitment?"

To what extent are you willing to agree to follow God's will before you know what that will might be?

However, it is not enough to know where we are called to share our gifts. We must also be committed to doing it. In fact, I believe that obedience comes before knowledge. I don't think we'll ever fully know God's will for our lives unless we first agree to follow it. When a decision arises in my life, I want to assess what my will is, what my family's will is, what the church might want, and finally what God might want me to do. God's will for my life is placed on the same level as all other competing claims, and I am still in charge of choosing what I will do. I want to remain in control. But Jesus calls us to seek first the kingdom of God and to trust that all these other matters will be cared for as well (Matthew 6:33). We are called to surrender our lives into God's hands without knowing where we will be led and to trust that God will care for all our other needs as well. Are we committed to doing the will of God? Once we say yes to that question, then we will discover what it is God calls us to be and do.

DISCUSSION POINT

What do you think—and feel—about this statement?

Several years ago, the congregation I served decided to send a mission work-team to Haiti to build a clinic at a mission compound. I was asked to be in charge of the team and to recruit the people necessary to accomplish the task. We had about a dozen wonderful volunteer workers, but none of us had the building and carpentry skills necessary to build a clinic facility. Consequently, I went to visit a contractor in our congregation to ask him to be on our team. After I had explained our request he said to me: "I don't even believe in missions. I think we should use our money to take care of needs right here at home. How do we know that the money we send overseas is not all wasted anyway? And you're asking me to give up two weeks of work and pay my own way to Haiti for a work project I'm not even sure I believe in." I said, "Yes, that's right." He said, "Let me think about it." The next day, he called me back and said that both he and his wife would be on the work-team, so they could see for themselves how mission funds were wasted.

We spent two weeks completing a clinic building at an isolated mountain village where there was no electricity or running water and all our food and supplies had to be hauled in. The clinic was next to a mission school where there were about 350 grade-school children attending classes each day. The principal of the school explained to us that most of the children in the school were malnourished and that you could tell when children were beginning to starve because the ends of their hair would begin to turn red. That meant they were not getting enough protein in their system to keep their hair black. Every day we saw numerous children with red tips to their hair.

Our contractor friend asked the principal why the school didn't provide a hot meal for these starving children each day. The principal explained that they used to do that. However, mission giving had declined, and now they could provide a meal only three or four times a month. The contractor said, "You mean if we don't give, they don't eat?" "That's right," replied the principal.

That experience affected our whole team profoundly, and particularly the contractor and his wife. When we returned to the United States, the contractor and his wife became strong advocates for mission support. They travelled all over our state showing slides, telling of the needs of children in Haiti, and raising thousands of dollars to provide a hot lunch program not only in that school but in all the mission schools in the region. They became mission coordinators and led two more mission teams to Haiti, two to Mexico, and three to the Rosebud Reservation in South Dakota.

When those two persons experienced the needs of children in Haiti personally and realized they had the God-given gifts to do something about it, they found their mission and ministry. They went on to make an incredible difference in the world. They saw very clearly where the needs of the world and their gifts and graces intersected. At that intersection they committed themselves to serving God and the world through this ministry.

Incidentally, they would say they are the ones who have been richly blessed and have grown in the faith. They have been privileged to learn from Christians who live in absolute poverty and retain their faith in Christ. We are all blessed when we commit ourselves to serving at the intersection between the desires of our hearts and the hungers of the world.

BIBLE STUDY

Read: 1 Corinthians 12-13 (Paul's Views on Gifts and Love)

We will use the Depth Bible Study method (also from *Teaching the Bible to Adults and Youth*, by Dick Murray) to explore Paul's discussion of spiritual gifts and the importance of love in 1 Corinthians 12 and 13. The Depth Bible Study method works like peeling the layers of an onion. We begin on the outside layer by seeking to understand what the text actually said in its own time and place. Then we peel back the next layer to ask what the passage says to us today. Finally, we get to the center and ponder what this passage means to me personally, asking, If I took this passage seriously, what changes would I make in my life? The closer we get to the center, the more we become personally involved. Just like peeling an onion, we could wind up in tears!

We should study chapters 12 and 13 of 1 Corinthians together because Paul writes about our individual spiritual gifts and our loving attitude toward others being in conjunction with one another. Years ago someone divided these ideas into the two chapters we have in the Bible. In Paul's original writing, however, they were not divided. One flowed into the other. Understanding our spiritual gifts and sharing them in love with others is essential in Paul's thinking.

Various competing groups divided the Christians in Corinth. Paul wrote to them both to affirm their diversity and to emphasize their unity in Christ. In the first chapter of 1 Corinthians, Paul discussed the divisions in the church between those who follow Apollos, or Peter, or Paul, or Christ. In chapters 12 and 13, Paul responded to those who felt their particular gift of the spirit was superior to others. Read through 1 Corinthians 12 and 13 and answer the following questions:

WRITTEN REFLECTION

1. Choose the verse or verses that you feel summarize best what Paul tried to convey to the Christians in Corinth.

2. In one sentence, put in your own words the essence of Paul's message to the Christians in Corinth.

3. What meaning does this passage have for us today?

4. What is the meaning of this passage for you? If you took this passage seriously, what changes would you make in your life?

GROUP INTERACTION

Ask group members to share their reflections in groups of three or four.

A national magazine sponsors an annual "Make a Difference Day" during which they encourage individuals and groups to do volunteer activities in their community that make life better for someone. In response, a group of about twenty women descended on a local nursing home. They volunteered to do whatever they could to make a difference in the lives of the residents and staff for one day. To do so, they wandered through the facility and did whatever needed doing. Some saw a broken fence in the back yard and repaired it. Others painted a bright mural of rainbows and flowers on it to brighten up the view of the residents who looked out on it daily. Yet others helped residents plant some bright flowers in the garden. Still others made a bright banner to hang in the dining hall. Some of the women gave facial massages to the women residents. Others sang songs and visited residents. Some helped clean the toilets and rooms of residents.

One of the volunteers shared with me the excitement she felt in simply making a commitment to make a difference. She spoke of how it seemed they were led to this nursing home and, without anyone telling anyone else what to do, they just began to use their gifts to meet the needs they saw. There just happened to be artists in the group to paint the mural and there just happened to be paint on hand with which to paint it. There happened to be fabric on hand and designers to make the banner. She was impressed that once they made the commitment, it was amazing how everything fell into place to accomplish the ministry.

DISCUSSION POINT

What do you think of this statement?

WRITTEN REFLECTION

The same thing is true in your life. Once you surrender your-self to God and take the leap of faith, heaven and earth shift and numerous "God-incidences" happen to enable you to ful-fill your ministries in Christ's name. The only thing that can hold you back is your refusal to commit. As you come to the end of this study, I invite you to commit yourself to following wherever Christ may lead you. You'll discover meaning in your life and joy beyond compare.

During this study, you have experienced some of the needs for healing and hope of persons in your church and in the world. You have also explored some of the gifts God has placed in your life. Now we want to see where those needs and gifts intersect. In the left-hand column below, list some needs of persons in your church and in the world. In the right-hand column list your gifts for ministry.

NEEDS OF PERSONS	MY GIFTS FOR MINISTRY
_____	_____
_____	_____
_____	_____
_____	_____
_____	_____
_____	_____
_____	_____
_____	_____
_____	_____

Once you've completed your lists, think about the relation-ship between the needs you've identified and the gifts you've been given. When you recognize a relationship between a need and a gift, draw a line from one to the other. These may be the places where God is calling you to ministry for the renewal of the church and for the transformation of the world.

WRITTEN REFLECTION

Decide on at least one area where needs and gifts intersect and make a commitment to begin ministry in that area. Write that one area here:

Decide that "if it's to be, it's up to me." God is waiting for your commitment. Once you've decided, you may need to visit with others about the most effective way of serving in a particular area, and you may need to further develop some of your God-given skills. But all of these considerations can be handled once you've made your commitment.

GROUP INTERACTION

Share your reflections with two or three other persons. Then, with the whole group, share where you've committed yourself to making a difference in the church and world.

DISCUSSION POINT

Be sure to spend ample time focusing on commitments persons want to make. But spend some time also on these questions: How might you talk yourself out of your commitment? How can you guard against this danger?

This public and open commitment is important lest you begin to talk yourself out of it as soon as this session is over. Remember, the Lord is sometimes described as the "hound of heaven" who keeps pursuing us and will not let us be content until we surrender control into God's hands and allow God to use our gifts in ministry to the needs of others for the salvation of the world.

WORSHIP

Conclude by praying the following covenant prayer. One church reformer, John Wesley, encouraged Christians to pray this prayer together regularly.

I am no longer my own, but thine.

Put me to what thou wilt, rank me with whom thou wilt. Put me to doing, put me to suffering.

Let me be employed by thee or laid aside for thee, exalted for thee or brought low by thee. Let me be full, let me be empty. Let me have all things, let me have nothing.

I freely and heartily yield all things to thy pleasure and disposal.

And now, O glorious and blessed God, Father, Son, and Holy Spirit, Thou art mine, and I am thine. So be it. And the covenant which I have made on earth, let it be ratified in heaven. Amen.

(From *The United Methodist Book of Worship.* Copyright © 1992 The United Methodist Publishing House, page 743.)

THE LifeSearch GROUP EXPERIENCE

Every LifeSearch group will be different. Because your group is made up of unique individuals, your group's experience will also be unique. No other LifeSearch group will duplicate the dynamics, feelings, and adventures your group will encounter.

And yet as we planned LifeSearch, we had a certain vision in mind about what we hoped might happen as people came together to use a LifeSearch book for discussion and support around a common concern. Each LifeSearch book focuses on some life concern of adults within a Christian context over a six-session course. LifeSearch books have been designed to be easy to lead, to encourage group nurture, and to be biblically based and needs-oriented.

Each chapter in this LifeSearch book has been designed for use during a one and one-half hour group session. In each LifeSearch book, you will find
• times for group members to "check in" with each other concerning what has gone on in their lives during the past week and what they wish to share from the past week concerning the material covered in the group sessions;
• times for group members to "check in" about how they are doing as a group;
• substantial information/reflection/discussion segments, often utilizing methods such as case studies and simulation;
• Bible study segments;
• segments in which a specific skill or process is introduced, tried out, and/or suggested for use during the week to come;
• segments that help group participants practice supporting one another with the concerns being explored.

LifeSearch was not planned with the usual one hour Sunday school class in mind. If you intend to use LifeSearch with a Sunday school class, you will need to adapt it to the length of time you have available. Either plan to take more than one week to discuss each chapter or be less ambitious with what you aim to accomplish in a session's time.

LifeSearch was also not planned to be used in a therapy group, a sensitivity group, or an encounter group.

No one is expected to be an expert on the topic. No one is expected to offer psychological insights into what is going on. However, we do hope that LifeSearch group members will offer one another support and Christian love.

We will count LifeSearch as successful if you find your way to thought-provoking discussions centered around information, insights, and helps providing aid for living everyday life as Christians.

You might find it helpful to see what we envisioned a sample LifeSearch group might experience. Keep in mind, however, that your experience might be quite different. Leave room for your creativity and uniqueness. Remain receptive to God's Spirit.

> A LifeSearch group is simply a group of persons who come together to struggle together from a Christian perspective with a common life concern.

You sit in the living room of a friend from church for the second session of your LIFESEARCH group. Besides you and your host, four other persons are present, sitting on the sofa and overstuffed chairs. You, your host, your group leader, and one other are church members, although not all of you make it to church that regularly. The remaining two persons are neighbors of the leader. You chat while a light refreshment and beverage are served by the host.

Your leader offers a brief prayer, and then asks each of you to share what has been going on in your lives during the past week since you last met. One member shares about a spouse who had outpatient surgery. Several mention how hectic the week was with the usual work- and family-related demands. Prayer concerns and requests are noted.

This session begins with a written reflection. The leader draws your attention to a brief question in the beginning of the chapter you were assigned to read for today. Group members are asked to think about the question and write a short response.

While the leader records responses on a small chalkboard brought for that purpose, members take turns sharing something from their written reflections. A brief discussion follows when one group member mentions something she had never noticed before.

Group members respond as the leader asks for any reports concerning trying out the new life skill learned in the previous session. Chuckles, words of encouragement, and suggestions for developing the new skill further pepper the reports.

The leader notes one of the statements made in the assigned chapter from the LIFESEARCH book and asks to what extent the statement is true to the experience of the group members. Not much discussion happens on this point, since everyone agrees the statement is true. But one of the members presses on to the next statement in the LIFESEARCH book, and all sorts of conversation erupts! All six group members have their hot buttons pushed.

Your leader calls the group to move on to Bible study time. You read over the text, and then participate in a dramatic reading in which everyone has a part. During the discussion that follows the reading, you share some insights that strike you for the first time because you identify with the person whose role you read.

You and the other group members take turns simulating a simple technique suggested in the book for dealing with a specific concern. Everyone coaches everyone else; and what could have been an anxiety-producing experience had you remained so self-conscious, quickly becomes both fun and helpful. You and one of the other group members agree to phone each other during the week to find out how you're doing with practicing this technique in real life.

It's a few minutes later than the agreed upon time to end, but no one seems to mind. You read together a prayer printed at the end of this week's chapter.

On the way out to your car, you ponder how quickly the evening has passed. You feel good about what you've learned and about deepening some new friendships. You look forward to the next time your LIFESEARCH group meets.

This has been only one model of how a LIFESEARCH group session might turn out. Yours will be different. But as you give it a chance, you will learn some things and you will deepen some friendships. That's what you started LIFESEARCH for anyway, isn't it?

STARTING A LifeSearch GROUP

The key ingredient to starting a LifeSearch group is *interest*. People are more likely to get excited about those things in which they are interested. People are more likely to join a group to study and to work on those areas of their lives in which they are interested.

Interest often comes when there is some itch to be scratched in a person's life, some anxiety to be soothed, or some pain to be healed.

Are persons interested in the topic of a LifeSearch book? Or, perhaps more important to ask, do they have needs in their lives that can be addressed using a LifeSearch book?

If you already have an existing group that finds interesting one of the topics covered by the LifeSearch books, go for it! Just keep in mind that LifeSearch is intended more as a small-group resource than as a class study textbook.

If you want to start a new group around LifeSearch, you can begin in one of two ways:

- You can begin with a group of interested people and let them choose from among the topics LifeSearch offers; or

- You can begin with one of the LifeSearch topics and locate people who are interested in forming a group around that topic.

What is the right size for a LifeSearch group? Well, how many persons do you have who are interested?

Actually, LifeSearch is intended as a *small-group* resource. The best size is between four and eight persons. Under four persons will make it difficult to carry out some of the group interactions. Over eight and not everyone will have a good opportunity to participate. The larger the group means the less time each person has to share.

If you have more than eight persons interested in your LifeSearch group, why not start two groups?

Or if you have a group larger than eight that just does not want to split up, then be sure to divide into smaller groups of no more than eight for discussion times. LifeSearch needs the kind of interaction and discussion that only happen in small groups.

How do you find out who is interested in LifeSearch? One good way is for you to sit down with a sheet of paper and list the names of persons whom you think might be interested. Even better would be for you to get one or two other people to brainstorm names with you. Then start asking. Call them on the telephone. Or visit them

> **Interest often comes when there is some itch to be scratched in a person's life, some anxiety to be soothed, or some pain to be healed.**

in person. People respond more readily to personal invitations.

When you invite persons and they seem interested in LIFESEARCH, ask them if they will commit to attending all six sessions. Emergencies do arise, of course. However, the group's life is enhanced if all members participate in all sessions.

LIFESEARCH is as much a group experience as it is a time for personal learning.

As you plan to begin a LIFESEARCH group, you will need to answer these questions:

• **Who will lead the group?** Will you be the leader for all sessions? Do you plan to rotate leadership among the group members? Do you need to recruit an individual to serve as group leader?

• **Where will you meet?** You don't have to meet at a church. In fact, if you are wanting to involve a number of persons not related to your church, a neutral site might be more appropriate. Why not hold your meetings at a home? But if you

do, make sure plans are made to hold distractions and interruptions to a minimum. Send the children elsewhere and put the answering machine on. Keep any refreshments simple.

• **How will you get the LIFESEARCH books to group members before the first session?** You want to encourage members to read the first chapter in advance of the first session. Do you need to have an initial gathering some days before the first discussion sessions in order to hand out books and take care of other housekeeping matters? Do you need to mail or otherwise transport the books to group members?

Most LIFESEARCH groups will last only long enough to work through the one LIFESEARCH book in which there is interest. Be open, however, to the possibility of either continuing your LIFESEARCH group as a support group around the life issue you studied, or as a group to study another topic in the LIFESEARCH series.

TIPS FOR LIVELY DISCUSSIONS

Don't lecture. You are responsible for leading a discussion, not for conveying information.

Ask open-ended questions. Ask: How would you describe the color of the sky? Don't ask: Is the sky blue?

Allow silence. Sometimes, some people need to think about something before they say anything. The WRITTEN REFLECTIONS encourage this kind of thought.

Recognize when the silence has gone on long enough. Some questions do fall flat. Some questions exhaust themselves. Some silence means that people really have nothing more to say. You'll come to recognize different types of silences with experience.

If Plan A doesn't work to stimulate lively discussion, move on to Plan B. Each chapter in this LIFESEARCH book contains more discussion starters and group interaction ideas than you can use in an hour and a half. If something doesn't work, move on and try something else.

Let the group lead you in leading discussion. Let the group set the agenda. If you lead the group in the direction you want to go, you might discover that no one is following you. You are leading to serve the group, not to serve yourself.

TIP 7

Ask follow-up questions. If someone makes a statement or offers a response, ask: Why do you say that? Better yet, ask a different group member: What do you think of so-and-so's statement?

TIP 8

Do your own homework. Read the assigned chapter. Plan out possible directions for the group session to go based on the leader's helps in the text. Plan options in case your first plan doesn't work out. Know the chapter's material.

TIP 9

Know your group. Think about the peculiar interests and needs of the specific individuals within your group. Let your knowledge of the group shape the direction in which you lead the discussion.

TIP 10

Don't try to accomplish everything. Each chapter in this LifeSearch book offers more leader's helps in the form of DISCUSSION POINTS, GROUP INTERACTIONS, and other items than you can use in one session. So don't try to use them all! People become frustrated with group discussions that try to cover too much ground.

TIP 11

Don't let any one person dominate the discussion—including yourself. (See "Dealing with Group Problems," page 58.")

TIP 12

Encourage, but don't force, persons who hold back from participation. (See "Dealing with Group Problems," page 58.)

TAKING YOUR GROUP'S TEMPERATURE

How do you tell if your LIFESEARCH group is healthy? If it were one human being, you could take its temperature with a thermometer and discover whether body temperature seemed to be within a normal range. Taking the temperature of a group is more complex and less precise. But you can try some things to get a sense of how healthily your group is progressing.

✓ **Find out whether the group is measuring up to what the members expected of it.** During the CHECKING IN portion of the first session, you are asked to record what members say as they share why they came to this LIFESEARCH group. At a later time you can bring out that sheet and ask how well the LIFESEARCH experience measures up to satisfying why people came in the first place.

✓ **Ask how members perceive the group dynamics.** Say: On a scale from one as the lowest to ten as the highest, where would you rate the overall participation by members of this group? On the same scale where would you rate this LIFESEARCH group as meeting your needs? On the same scale where would you rate the "togetherness" of this LIFESEARCH group?

You can make up other appropriate questions to help you get a sense of the temperature of the group.

✓ **Ask group members to fill out an evaluation sheet on the LIFESEARCH experience.** Keep the evaluation form simple.

One of the simplest forms leaves plenty of blank space for responding to three requests: (1) Name the three things you would want to do more of. (2) Name the three things you would want to do less of. (3) Name the three things you would keep about the same.

✓ **Debrief a LIFESEARCH session with one of the other participants.** Arrange ahead of time for a group member to stay a few minutes after a meeting or to meet with you the next day. Ask for direct feedback about what seemed to work or not work, who seems to be participating well, who seems to be dealing with something particularly troubling, and so forth.

✓ **Give group members permission to say when they sense something is not working.** As the group leader, you do not hold responsibility for the life of the group. The group's life belongs to *all* the members of the group. Encourage group members to take responsibility for what takes place within the group session.

✓ **Expect and accept that, at times, discussion starters will fall flat, group interaction will seem stilted, group members will be grumpy**. All groups have bad days. Moreover all groups go through their own life cycles. Although six sessions may not be enough time for your LIFESEARCH group to gel completely, you may find that after two or three sessions, one session will come when nothing seems to go right. That is normal. In fact, studies show that only those groups that first show a little conflict ever begin to move into deeper levels of relationship.

✔ **Sit back and observe.** In the middle of a DISCUSSION POINT or GROUP INTER-ACTION, sit back and try to look at the group as a whole. Does it look healthy to you? Is one person dominating? Does someone else seem to be withdrawn? How would you describe what you observe going on within the group at that time?

✔ **Take the temperature of the group—really!** No, not with a thermometer. But try asking the group to take its own temperature. Would it be normal? below normal? feverish? What adjective would you use to describe the group's temperature?

✔ **Keep a temperature record.** At least keep some notes from session to session on how you think the health of the group looks to you. Then after later sessions, you can look back on your notes from earlier sessions and see how your group has changed.

LIFESEARCH Group Temperature Record

Chapter 1
_____
_____
_____
_____

Chapter 4
_____
_____
_____
_____

Chapter 2
_____
_____
_____
_____

Chapter 5
_____
_____
_____
_____

Chapter 3
_____
_____
_____
_____

Chapter 6
_____
_____
_____
_____

DEALING WITH GROUP PROBLEMS

What do you do if your group just does not seem to be working out?

First, figure out what is going on. The ideas in "Taking Your Group's Temperature" (pages 56-57) will help you to do this. If you make the effort to observe and listen to your group, you should be able to anticipate and head off many potential problems.

Second, remember that the average LIFE-SEARCH group will only be together for six weeks—the average time needed to study one LIFESEARCH book. Most new groups will not have the chance to gel much in such a short period of time. Don't expect the kind of group development and nurture you might look for in a group that has lived and shared together for years.

Third, keep in mind that even though you are a leader, the main responsibility for how the group develops belongs to the group itself. You do the best you can to create a hospitable setting for your group's interactions. You do your homework to keep the discussion and interactions flowing. But ultimately, every member of the group individually and corporately bear responsibility for whatever happens within the life of the group.

However, if these specific problems do show up, try these suggestions:

✓ One Member Dominates the Group

• Help the group to identify this problem for itself by asking group members to state on a scale from one as the lowest to ten as the highest where they would rank overall participation within the group.

• Ask each member to respond briefly to a DISCUSSION POINT in a round robin fashion. It may be helpful to ask the member who dominates to respond toward the end of the round robin.

• Practice gate-keeping by saying, "We've heard from Joe; now what does someone else think?"

• If the problem becomes particularly troublesome, speak gently outside of a group session with the member who dominates.

✓ One Member Is Reluctant to Participate

• Ask each member to respond briefly to a DISCUSSION POINT in a round robin fashion.

• Practice gate-keeping for reluctant participants by saying, "Sam, what would you say about this?"

• Increase participation by dividing the larger group into smaller groups of two or three persons.

✓ The Group Chases Rabbits Instead of Staying With the Topic

• Judge whether the rabbit is really a legitimate or significant concern for the group to be discussing. By straying from your agenda, is the group setting an agenda more valid for their needs?

• Restate the original topic or question.

• Ask why the group seems to want to avoid a particular topic or question.

• If one individual keeps causing the group to stray inappropriately from the topic, speak with him or her outside of a session.

✔ Someone Drops Out of the Group

• A person might drop out of the group because his or her needs are not being met within the group. You will never know this unless you ask that person directly.

• Contact a person immediately following the first absence. Otherwise they are unlikely to return.

✔ The Group or Some of Its Members Remain on a Superficial Level of Discussion

• In a six-session study, you cannot necessarily expect enough trust to develop for a group to move deeper than a superficial level.

• Never press an individual member of a LIFESEARCH group to disclose anything more than they are comfortable doing so in the group.

• Encourage an atmosphere of confidentiality within the group. Whatever is said within the group, stays within the group.

✔ Someone Shares a Big, Dangerous, or Bizarre Problem

• LIFESEARCH groups are not therapy groups. You should not take on the responsibility of "fixing" someone else's problem.

• Encourage a member who shares a major problem to seek professional help.

• If necessary, remind the group about the need for confidentiality.

• If someone shares something that endangers either someone else or himself/herself, contact your pastor or a professional caregiver (psychologist, social worker, physician, attorney) for advice.

IF YOU'RE NOT LEADING THE GROUP

> Be sure to read this article if you are *not* the person with specific responsibility for leading your LifeSearch group.

If you want to get the most out of your LifeSearch group and this LifeSearch book, try the following suggestions.

✓ **Make a commitment to attend all the group sessions and participate fully.** An important part of the LifeSearch experience takes place within your group. If you miss a session, you miss out on the group life. Also, your group will miss what you would have added.

✓ **Read the assigned chapter in your LifeSearch book ahead of time.** If you are familiar with what the MAIN TEXT of the LifeSearch book says, you will be able to participate more fully in discussions and group interactions.

✓ **Try the activities suggested in BEFORE NEXT TIME.** Contributions you make to the group discussion based upon your experiences will enrich the whole group. Moreover, LifeSearch will only make a real difference in your life if you try out new skills and behaviors outside of the group sessions.

✓ **Keep confidences shared within the group.** Whatever anyone says within the group needs to stay within the group. Help make your group a safe place for persons to share their deeper thoughts, feelings, and needs.

✓ **Don't be a "problem" participant.** Certain behaviors will tend to cause difficulties within the life of any group. Read the article on "Dealing with Group Problems," on pages 58-59. Do any of these problem situations describe you? Take responsibility for your own group behavior, and change your behavior as necessary for the sake of the health of the whole group.

✓ **Take your turn as a group leader, if necessary.** Some LifeSearch groups will rotate group leadership among their members. If this is so for your LifeSearch group, accept your turn gladly. Read the other leadership articles in the back of this LifeSearch book. Relax, do your best, and have fun leading your group.

✓ **Realize that all group members exercise leadership within a group.** The health of your group's life belongs to all the group members, not just to the leader alone. What can you do to help your group become healthier and more helpful to its members? Be a "gatekeeper" for persons you notice are not talking much. Share a thought or a feeling if the discussion is slow to start. Back off from sharing your perspective if you sense you are dominating the discussion.

✓ **Take responsibility for yourself.** Share concerns, reflections, and opinions related to the topic at hand as appropriate. But keep in mind that the group does not exist to "fix" your problems. Neither can you "fix" anyone else's problems, though from time to time it may be appropriate to share insights on what someone else is facing based upon your own experience and wisdom. Instead of saying, "What you need to do is . . ." try saying, "When I have faced a similar situation, I have found it helpful to . . ."

✓ **Own your own statements.** Instead of saying, "Everyone knows such and so is true," try saying "I believe such and so is true, because . . . ." Or instead of saying "That will never work," try saying, "I find it hard to see how that will work. Can anyone help me see how it might work?" Instead of saying, "That's dumb!" try saying, "I have a hard time accepting that statement because . . . ."

OUR LifeSearch GROUP

Name	Address	Phone Number

FEEDBACK MAIL-IN SHEET

✂ CUT HERE

Please tell us what you liked and disliked about LIFESEARCH:

4. The two things I like best about this LIFESEARCH experience were

5. The two things I liked least about this LIFESEARCH experience were

6. The two things I would have done differently if I had designed this LIFESEARCH book are

7. Topics for which you should develop new LIFE-SEARCH books are

8. I want to be sure to say the following about LIFE-SEARCH.

9. I led _____ sessions of this LIFESEARCH book.

FOLD HERE

Thank you for taking the time to fill out and return this feedback questionnaire.

Please check the LIFESEARCH book you are evaluating.

☐ Spiritual Gifts   ☐ Health and Wholeness
☐ Juggling Demands ☐ Stress
☐ Parenting   ☐ The Environment

Please tell us about your group:

1. Our group had an average attendance of _____.

2. Our group was made up of
_____ young adults (19 through 25 years of age).
_____ adults mostly between 25 and 45 years of age.
_____ adults mostly between 45 and 60 years of age.
_____ adults 60 and over.
_____ a mixture of ages.

3. Our group (answer as many as apply)
_____ came together for the sole purpose of studying this LIFESEARCH book.
_____ has decided to study another LIFESEARCH book.
_____ is an ongoing Sunday school class.
_____ met at a time other than Sunday morning.
_____ had only one leader for this LIFESEARCH study.

Name_____

Address_____

_____

Telephone_____

PLACE
STAMP
HERE

Editor, LifeSearch series
Church School Publications
P. O. Box 801
Nashville, Tennessee 37202

STAPLE OR TAPE HERE